The Story Behind My

Smile

Dr. Sandra Withers

Copyright © 2022
Withers Publishing West Covina, CA
979-8-88757-743-2

Layout Design: Inkcept Studio
Book Project Management—Start Write Publish
contact@startwriteaway.com
http://startwriteaway.com
Start Write Team
Editors: Dr. Gerald C. Simmons & Dr. Cherie Graham
Editorial Assistants: Jennifer Eiland & Tiara Martin Brown
Front/Back Cover: Rainah Davis

TABLE OF CONTENTS

ACKNOWLEDGEMENT

I would like to express my deepest appreciation to my husband, Michael Withers who has been exceptionally patient throughout the writing of this book. He continually and convincingly conveyed abiding support throughout this undertaking, without his persistent encouragement this book would not have been possible.

In addition, I would like to give a big shout out to my adult children, Maxine Thompson and Nathan Pollonais for their enthusiasm in seeing my story come alive. Your patience will always have a lasting effect on me.

Finally, thanks to my deceased mother, Vera Lumpress, and deceased brother, Bernard Saline, your influence will continue to fearlessly propel me into territories unknown.

Chapter 1:

FACTS ABOUT A SMILE

Webster's *Dictionary* defines a smile as a "pleasant, kind, or an amused facial expression where the corners of the mouth are typically turned upwards, the front teeth are exposed, the cheeks are raise and the skin around the eyes bunches up." Smiles do make differences in the lives of people. Not only does it make a difference, but it also serves as a symbol of inclusion and friendship, which makes life more meaningful.

Complex brain activities take place when a person smiles, one of which is the waning of stress. Even at a time when a person is not able to, or prefers not to smile, if he or she can forge a smile, they more than likely can walk away feeling better about their situation(s). In addition, a smile causes people to appear attractive to others; the gesture suggests that someone is easy-going, personable, or caring in nature. Subsequently, people are predisposed to approach someone who wears a smile.

When a person is crying, the people around them are prone to share in the emotion and weep with them. Smiles tend to emit a similar emotional reaction because they both have an infectiousness about them. Smiles are extremely powerful in that they have the ability to lift the spirit of others. It is also noteworthy to mention that a smile can represent a number of emotion, such as, anxiety, fear, joy and satisfaction based on cultural interpretations.

Growing up in Trinidad, I was blessed to have my mother and my older brother who showered me with love and cultivated in me a sense of self and communal living. However, because I lived in an extended family, and finances was scarce, life's experiences were extremely challenging at times; but for the most part life was exciting and unpredictable. The adults in my extended family were responsible for my care and discipline, which included correcting and/or spanking when there was misbehavior or retaliation.

My dad was an absentee father, but my brother, who was five years my senior, along with my grandfather on my mother's side appropriated the role of father figures in my life. For a number of years, I thought that my brother was indeed my father, and I respected and honored him. However, when I found out later on that he was not my father, but my brother, I experienced a freedom around him and embraced him accordingly.

I had a very meager upbringing; our house was built from a mixture of mud, straw, and cow dung or manure, food was scarce, and money was even scarcer. Nevertheless, the sparseness in my life had little to no effect on my mental and emotional well-being. My upbringing was primarily about family, hard work, play, and laughter. However, something was missing; it was the presence and love of a father.

Around the age of six, I began to ask questions such as, "Who is my dad, and why was he not living in the home with me?" These questions became particularly overwhelming to me in my school age years since my friends were constantly raving about their parents, in particular, their dads. The questions I posed to my mother and brother about my father were frequent, lengthy and sincere. I wanted to know more about my dad and why he was not present to care for me. Every morning as I entered the school grounds, I would see fathers dropping off their children, exchanging hugs and smiles, and I wondered what life would be like if my father was only in it.

It became increasingly obvious that my mother and brother did not have the answers to my questions and that I would not be able to share in this father-daughter experience I craved. Nonetheless, the nagging images of fathers hugging and smiling with their children preoccupied my mind to the extent that I yearned even more to share in the experience. The thought of which mercilessly obsessed my mind.

Apart from the apparent pain of not having my father in the home, I had a casual lifestyle that brought with it excitement, inquisitiveness, playfulness, and fleeting ease. Happiness came from the satisfaction of having my mother, brother, relatives, friends, communal sharing, story-telling, backyard gardening, and sporting activities. Though simple as it seems, each experience afforded me a sense of contentment that brought about a smile. People in the community would describe me as "the child who was always smiling."

For the most part, Trinidadians are a gentle and a happy-go-lucky group of people with smiles that "light up a room." Having a big smile is common among the natives because they are taught never to wear their feelings on their sleeves. Smiles for some was a way to cover up their true feelings, whatever the reason behind the smile, they were common and strikingly present on the faces of the people. A smile on the faces of a Trinidadian greatly contributed to the perceived climate of the culture.

A little known fact is that Trinidadians are a patriotic people who does not equate their nationality or cultural identification with ethnicity but with their citizenship. The natives are extremely loyal and, refer to themselves as "Trinidadian to the bone." Tourists from around the world rush to Trinidad to enjoy the food, music, beaches, and, most of all, the sociability of the people. How we Trinidadians have come to identify ourselves seems to be unimportant to the tourists, they embraced and enjoyed the warmth of the people and the culture.

Chapter 2

GROWING UP TRINIDADIAN (TRINI)

As mentioned earlier, I was born and raised on the tropical Island of Trinidad and Tobago, which is one of the southernmost islands in the Caribbean Sea. It is the fifth largest island in the West Indies and consists of an area of 4,768 km². It lies 11 km off the northeastern coast of Venezuela and sits on the continental shelf of South America. Though geographically part of the South American continent, from a socio-economic standpoint, Trinidad is often referred to as the southernmost island in the Caribbean.

*Illustration 1: Map of Trinidad and Tobago
showing Proximity to Venezuela*

English is the preferred language in Trinidad, followed by Spanish and a version of French, referred to as "patois." The food and music have its influence by cultures, such as, Indian, African, Amerindian, Portuguese, Spanish, and Chinese; however, Trinidadians have developed its unique "flavor," style of cooking, and genre of music. Some of the most common foods are callaloo, which a potpourri of green vegetables, the leaves of the taro plant, ochra,

pumpkin, coconut milk, and local seasonings. Coo Coo, a creole version of polenta and is made from corn, coconut milk, local seasonings and ochre, based on preference. The people enjoy the calypso music, and the percussion instrument of choice is the steel pan. Winston Spree was accredited as its pioneer.

Respect for one's elders is high regarded on the cultural "totem pole." As a child, I clearly remember that one rule that was seriously highlighted in our home was respect for elders. Children were taught very early to respond to adults with the phrase, "Yes sir," or "Yes ma'am." Teachers were addressed as "Sir, Mrs. or Miss."

Children dared not refer to a female adult as "she." If the word "she" was used to address any adult female and my mother, or another adult would hear it, it was frowned upon, considered to be disrespectful and had severe consequence, such as, a spanking. The adult would quickly interrupt the children's conversation by looking at child sternly and asking, "Who is 'She, the cat's mother?"

To this day, I still cannot fathom its meaning. The disconcerting part of the situation is that children were not allowed to question adults and, therefore, would refrain from asking for an explanation. Primarily due to fear of repercussions, such as a spanking. The tone in their adult voices and the look in their eyes, quieted the curiosity in such a child, they knew they were in trouble and would quickly address the adult appropriately without asking for a reason for the outrage.

The norm among locals with regard to greetings was simple, hail each person with "good morning" or "good afternoon" depending on the time of day. Respect was intensely entrenched in the people. This custom was without prejudice of color, creed, or religion. Every adult in the community had the responsibility of raising and disciplining the children of that community and to instill aspects of the culture that were non-negotiable. These responsibilities ranged from respect to spanking, spanking to feeding and being each other's neighbor.

Then there was the careless ease of locals. There exists a sense of ease among locals, not in work ethics or education, but towards leisure. The saying, "All work and no play makes Jack a dull boy" is a running theme among the hard-working people of Trinidad. When it was time to embracing leisure, it was a priority. It is a time to eat, drink and be merry. Businesses in the country are closed, natives can either be spectators or they can join in the fun. The phrase "Trinidad time" or "we time," have to do with unparalleled non-commitment to timeliness, rather, natives are known to be tardy. The motto is either all work, or all play.

Carnival in Trinidad takes place on the Monday and Tuesday before Lent with "fetes," parties, dance, and calypso music. A good example of the need for festivities is Trinidad Carnival, the country would participate in two days of festivities, but in reality, parties can last up to two weeks. During the Christmas season, the festivities continues with "parang" music which originated from Venezuela. Families and other large groups would gather to celebrate the birth of Jesus with food, song, dance.

Trinidadians embrace and strongly uphold a close-knit culture that is reflective in the national motto: "Together we aspire, together we achieve." The national anthem features the line, "Here every creed and race find an equal place," and is sung twice for emphasis, for it endorses the abiding sense of oneness and unity that is shared among the people.

In this culture, older siblings, relatives, and neighbors play significant roles in nurturing, caring, and disciplining children, hence the term, "a village is responsible to raise a child." "Back chat," or talking back to parents or adults is something that is simply not tolerated in this culture. Children were expected to show "broughtupsy," or respect toward adults at all times; there were simply no room for slip-ups. The ubiquitous idea about children was that they should be seen and not heard, so the children observed from a distance.

The culture in Trinidadian places a high importance on education. Family members and relatives alike make great sacrifices to support their children in reaching their educational potentials. I grew up in an extended family, which included my grandfather (on my mother's side of the family), mother, older brother, aunts, uncles and cousins. My grandfather and my brother (who was five years my senior), played the role of "father figure," as mentioned earlier. They insisted on study time, homework, and reading at least one book a day.

Whether my family and/or extended family had to sell a cow, goat or sheep to pay for my education, the decision was simple. Everyone would do their part in order to meet my family's expectation of me, which was to graduate from primary school, enter high school, or "college" (as they referred to high school in Trinidad) and/or pursue higher education. Education was a huge priority because the culture dictated that children was to care for their parents in their older years. The parents' home assumed priority over their children's.

Trinidad is also known for its religiosity and religious diversities. The majority of the population in recent years are Indians, their religious persuasion is a mix between Hinduism and Muslim religion; the rest of the community are Christians. I grew up in a household where Catholicism was observed. Every Sunday my mother walked several miles to get to the one Catholic Church and my brother and I were expected to accompany her. It was while attending a Sunday service that the Holy Spirit began prompting me into a relationship with Jesus Christ. As I walked home after service, I began to bombard my mother with questions about God and faith. Indeed, God was preparing me for what was to come.

Life was overwhelmingly challenging for my family, my mother had only a third grade education and was barely able to make ends meet. She was a seamstress; the only one in the neighbor who would sew clothing. She would sew adult and children's clothing and sell them to families in the community; but, since resources were scarce, months would pass before she would receive payments for her services.

As word of her skill as a seamstress noised about, my mother landed a contract with Woolworth, a large retail clothing company in the area. The company agreed to sell her clothing in their store, but fate would have it that she had to wait sometimes for up to three months before the she received payments for her service (s).

After my youngest aunt (the last of my mother's female sibling) migrated to Canada, she sent a twenty-dollar Canadian bill to my mother on a monthly basis to assist my mother with her household expenses. My mother used a portion of the money (the exchange rate was approximately $120.00 in Trinidadian dollars) to pay my school fees of twenty-five Trinidadian dollars a month at the neighboring Seventh-day Adventist school which was a stone's throw away from our home.

Our home was a mud shack, which was made from a mixing of mud, straw, cow dung and water to form a cement-like consistency. The frame of the house was made from pieces of sticks and limbs of trees. The cement-like mixture held the pieces of sticks in place to form the walls of the house. The Trinidadian term for the application of the mud and cow dung mixture is the term "Lipay. Not only did this mud mixture cover the walls of the house, but it also covered the floor of the house creating uniformity to the flooring space."

The roof of the mud shack was covered with dried coconut branches which created a tighter, more stable covering rather than the green leaves of the coconut tree. My brother and I helped my mother build the structure as she toiled tirelessly to cover the roof of the house in anticipation of the rainy season. My mother, brother and I lived in the finished section of the house until the rest of the house was completed. My mother's words were, "We will make do," What she meant was the family would make themselves comfortable until a better way of life can be afforded. As the sun dried the walls of the structure, it looked rather welcoming.

The inside of the house was warm or hot in the summer months and cool or cold in the rainy months. However, the biggest concern during torrential rains was that the "Lipay" walls would erode, but even more significant, our family would not have shelter. Strange enough, there would always be a portion of the house that would stand during the rainy months. I was questioned by friends about the odor of the dung on more than one occasion. I must confess that as hard as I tried, I still cannot recall an odor coming from the cow dung mixture, which covered the walls of our home.

As custom had it, I had to read a book daily, if possible, so I would sit in the corner of the mud house surrounded by my second-hand books, which my mother secured prior to going to another grade. She would use the barter system at the end of each semester and trade books for clothing which she had sown to family, friends or neighbors. (Barter system is the exchanging of goods or services between two or more people without the use of money). Since money was scare, and she did not have the money to buy new books, it was a good way to achieve this end.

I would light the wick of a flambeau (a half-filled bottle with kerosene with a wick which was lit to give light) with a match and read for hours. When I was through reading, I would memorize difficult words from my torn dictionary. I enjoyed reading, learning new words, and spelling so much that I would read the same book over and over again. This intellectual indulgence was my "me time."

Since the house had no electricity, the flambeau provided the family with light both inside the house and around the house to scare off wild animals, and other preys. If I was reading a very interesting book into the late hours of the evening, I would hold the flambeau in one hand and read until I was ready to sleep. The sad part was when there was no money to buy kerosene; my mother would use candles or have us go to bed early to accommodate the darkness. The only access my family had with the outside world was listening to the news on her small radio early in the morning or at nights. Apart from this small radio, (which would work only when my mother could afford to purchase batteries), my family had no contact with the outside world.

Nights at our home were particularly hot and extremely challenging. My mother, brother, and I slept on a fiber mattress on a wooden bunk bed in a small bedroom which was walled off from the rest of the house. As soon as the light from the flambeau went out, it was "party time" for the bed bugs and sheer agony for all three of us, my mother, brother and me. The bugs came out in great numbers and fed on our blood. I could not be comforted; my mother would encourage me to try falling asleep.

In fierce retaliation, my mother would pounce on several bugs at a time as they crawl around on the mattress. In one sweep of her hands she would kill a number of them. Although this approach was grossed me out, I welcomed her every attempt to get rid of the bugs so that I could fall asleep. But even her most resolute efforts were not good enough to keep the bugs from coming out in numbers at nights. In the mornings when I rose from the bed, there would be multiple visible red lesions from the bite marks on my skin and blisters from scratching them.

Illustration 2: Flambeau

Upon waking up at five in the mornings, I would be required to lead the cows and goats to the pasture, sweep around the mud shack, wash myself, (usually with a full bucket of water that was sitting out through the day before in the sun), eat whatever was available, then head out to school. I would also be required to fill a barrel with water from a nearby standpipe (a water pipe connected to a reservoir) if the barrels of water at the house were running low. Each person in the house, excluding my mother and grandfather, would take turns filling barrels with water from the standpipe as soon as they were getting low. My mother emphatically stated that the household should never be without water.

I would place the barrel on a wooden cart with four wheels (See illustration below) with the help of my brother. Attached to the cart was a rope, which allowed my brother and I to pull the cart through the street. My brother would assist me to pull the cart and barrel if he was through with his chores, even if it was not his turn to fill the barrel with water. Together we would pull the cart with the full barrel of water, my brother would make a tedious task exciting. He had a glowing personality and a caring spirit. He truly cared for me, he would make me laugh, when I did not feel like laughing and would do whatever he could to make life a bit more tolerable for me.

One day while I was sitting at my desk at primary school, I saw a man walking towards the school building. He had an average size and height, hard curly and light skin tone. He beckoned my teacher Ms. Bartholomew, stating that he was at the school to visit with me and claiming to be my father. Ms. Bartholomew had a quizzical look on her face, but the man insisting he was my father and wanted to talk with me.

I was in shock, but curiosity took the better part of me because I had never seen my father. My eyes welded up with tears, I wanted to hug the man and called him "Daddy." I just could not control my tears. Ms. Bartholomew asked me if I knew the man standing in front of me and I said, "No. I do not know him." The man pleaded with my teacher to speak to me. His pleas touched her, so she agreed to let him speak to me and reassured me that she would be present throughout the talk.

With tears in my eyes, I reluctantly walked toward the man. Upon meeting with this stranger, he told me that he was my father, and reached out his hand to shake mine. I refused to shake his hand. He then handed me a small brown paper bag which I nervously took and opened. Inside the bag was a variety of candies. The man, my "father" said, "Go ahead, have one," but I would not dare. After his failed attempts to have me partake of a candy, he tried to engage me in other conversations, like, "How was I doing" I was lost for words and could not speak. I muttered to myself, "I do not have a father." Where was he all these years? The man then left the school and I watched as he slowly walked away.

The day seemed to move along rather quickly. My mother showed up at the end of the school day as she always does to escort me home. My teacher relayed the story of the unannounced visit from this stranger to my mother. She was obviously upset by the news, and told Ms. Bartholomew, my teacher that she should not have allowed me to speak to him, especially since she was not aware of his visit and had not given permission.

On our way home, mother said very firmly, "I told you not to speak to strangers." I apologized and then handed her the bag of candies that my visitor (father) had given to me. My mother forcefully grabbed the bag from my hands and placed them in her small handbag. From that moment on, I never laid eyes on the bag, much less the candies that were in it. How I wished I could have tasted at least one of them.

Life continued, but I always thought of the man who said he was my father. One late afternoon while my brother and I were going to the neighboring standpipe to fill a barrel with water, I had a severe accident, I was about ten years old at the time. My brother was pulling the cart at top speed, I was standing on the back of the cart holding onto the barrel as he careened down the incline.

My brother jumped on the cart as it precipitously rolled down the incline. Little did my brother or I know that the day the city workers had dug up the street and had left exposed boulders lying around for the following day. As we sped down the incline on the way to the stand pipe, I tumbled over the empty barrel, and the cart went in a different direction, which caused me to land face down on a boulder.

My brother and my thought that day was like every other day; we were going to get some fun out of the ride as we do our chore. However; the difference was clear, it was not the break of dawn when he would have the sun peeping out at us, it was approaching evening and the sun was going down. To make matters worse, there were no street lights to make up for the deficit. My brother and I were certainly oblivious of the danger lying ahead.

After falling on to the bolder, I lost consciousness, when I came through, I called out to my brother, "brother where are you?" He answered, "Where are you?" I told him that I had fallen and could not get up. He followed the sound of my voice and found me. I tried standing up, but I could not because my right knee was in excruciating pain. I brushed my hand over the painful area on my knee, and felt a warm thick liquid running down my leg. I panicked as I yelled to my brother, "Lift me up and take me home." He wasted no time in lifting me off the street, and ran with me as fast as he could to our home.

When we arrived at our home, my brother sat me down on the broken-down living room couch and with a loud voice called out to my mother. She quickly ran into the room with a flambeau in hand, and screamed as she saw blood flowing everywhere: on my clothes, inside my shoes, and on the couch. My mother was in shock, and was unable to utter a word she began pacing the floor of the living room, and with tears running down her cheeks, she cried, "Lord, can you tell me what to do?" She readied herself in

some reasonable clothing and ran through the front door.

It seemed as though my mother re-entered the front door as quickly as she went out. As I looked out the front door, I saw the silhouette of a car somewhat white in color parked at the entrance to our house. The driver of the car came out the car and began approaching the house. Once inside the house, the driver and my brother carried me to the car. Together they guided both feet and sat me in an upright position on the back seat of the car. My mother propped me up with clothing and other pieces of rags she found in the car to support me as I sat up against the seat.

The driver entered the driver's seat and my mother entered the passenger seat respectfully my brother, returned to the house. From the front seat of the car my mother comforted me by telling me everything would be all right. However, when she told me that she was taking me to the hospital, I was scared beyond measure and began crying aloud. I asked her if she would stay with me at the hospital, she assured me that she was going to stay with me and I felt comforted by her words.

On arrival at the hospital, I was rushed into the emergency room and was prepped for surgery. I remembered being rolled into surgery on a gurney and being placed under a huge bright light. The next morning, I was lying on a hospital bed that was surrounded by side rails. A number of children were lying in adjacent beds; some were playing on the floor, while a group of men and women wearing white uniforms were hustling and bustling around the room.

One of the ladies in white approached my bed, and I began screaming at the top of my lungs. She oriented and reassured me as she spoke her name, and told me she was my nurse and would be caring for me. She explained to me that I was in the hospital because of a fractured knee. She further informed me that there were other children on the unit, I was not alone, and that the nurses would bring me breakfast shortly.

She also volunteered some additional information that piqued my interest: she told me that my mother would be back soon to be with me.

The thought of my mother "being back soon" comforted me, so I regained my composure, wiped my eyes, and trusted the words from this lady in white attire. Later that day, my mother entered the room; her entrance was a breath of fresh air. She looked tired, but when she saw me, she lit up and gave me a huge and reassuring smile that quieted her frightened daughter. I smiled back at her and leaned forward on both elbows. She bent over as well, kissed me, and handed me a small bag of candies. I opened the bag and was surprised by the assortment. I gave her a big smile.

My mother visited me every day for three months in the hospital and brought me bag of candy every week. I appreciated her so much for being so selfless. I knew she did not have the money to keep visiting me and bringing me candies, but she somehow made it happen for me. My mother was the dearest and kindest person I knew. She was my mentor, and I loved her with all my heart.

I was required by the staff to lie in the supine position on the hospital bed in an effort to keep my fractured knee cap in alignment in order to promote healing. The cast on my right leg had an iron rod peeking out on both sides at the knee. Attached to the iron rod was a rope about one-quarter of an inch in width. The rope draped over the footboard of my hospital bed and held two sandbags in place that were attached at the end of the rope. The doctor explained to my mother that the bags were in position to keep my knee in alignment.

Not only was this set-up uncomfortable, it was inconvenient, I was unable to go to the bathroom, but would use a bath pan with the help of a nurse. I was unable to run around and play like the other children. I felt restricted by both the fracture and the contraption because together they both rendered me bed bound. In tandem, I felt slighted by the kids who were able to walk around because they ignored me.

As I lay on my bed contemplating my demise, thoughts of the man who called himself my father at school ran through my mind and it made me extremely sad and angry. The thoughts of not having my father at my side, plagued me. However, I was happier when the afternoon came around because I would see my mother and occasionally my older brother. I learned to mask the pain around my family members. After three months as an in-patient at the hospital, I was discharged and returned home to recuperate.

Life continued along as usual but at the age of seventeen, the pain of not knowing or having my dad around overwhelmed me. It prompted me to pay him a visit so I asked a few friends at my church to accompany me on a visit to my dad. I received directions from my dad to my dad's house, and we ventured out.

His house was in the north western section of Trinidad. a far distance from where I lived with my mother and brother. Even though the proposed journey would be my second meeting with the man who visited me at school and called himself my dad. I was excited about visiting him since during this visit I would demand answers to my many questions. I was excited, but equally apprehensive about the meeting.

When my friends and I arrived at the location, we questioned the locals about his whereabouts, and they gave us directions to his home. The directions led us to a dark dirt track in a forested area. Dirt tracks are not uncommon to people living in Trinidad. The path we were on was dark, there were no street lights, only the light from the setting sun, and later on a torchlight that we had in our possession. It was also scary because we heard weird sound around us. We walked for about what seemed to be an hour and almost gave up hope before we saw a wooden shack with a barbed-wire fence that fitted the description given to us by the locals.

As we approached the house, I ran up to the gate, shaking it and shouting as loud as I can, "Daddy, daddy, this is Sandy. I am here to see you." I saw eyes peering over the curtain from the one window facing the gate. There was no response, so I shouted louder, "Daddy, daddy, this is Sandy, I am here to see you." I shouted one more time, and then a voice shouted back at me, "I do not know a Sandy." I replied, "Do you know Sandra, your daughter?" He replied, "I do not have a daughter." My heart sank within me. I replied, "Daddy, but you came to see me at school a long time ago. I am older now, and I came to see you." He responded, "The same way you came, take the trail and go right back." Then, the eyes that were peering over the curtain disappeared.

I stood at the gate in total shock as I tried to make sense of what had just happened. As I stood there in silence, I heard the sound of thunder and saw a flash of lightning in the distance. I lifted my head to dark thick clouds in the sky and felt big rain drops pouring down my body. I begged my father to let us in to take cover from the rain, he refused. As I reluctantly walked away from my daddy's' house I was in total shock.

The way out was filled with silence, one of my friends walked to the side of me, the other followed close behind me. None of my friends said a word, it seemed as though they did not have the right words to say to me. It was an extremely unpleasant situation, and the walk to the entrance seemed like a life time. The tears poured down my face because I was full of grief.

My emotions were running wild; I just could not be comforted. The only consolation was the darkness of the night hid my tears from my friends. I cringed as I realize that soon my friends and I would be at the entrance of the path, and the street lights would reveal my swollen eyes from the tears I had shed over the past hour.

I had high hopes that I would at least have my questions answered, but it seemed as though all hope was gone. Hope has a dark side in the way it impacts the mind because its intensity and dominance is like a mental prison. I asked myself, "Was all hope gone?" At least so it seemed. There were no words to describe the emptiness I felt on the inside. I was hopeful that something good would have taken place during the visit with my dad, but the worse let down took place. I was convinced that there had to be an antidote for the rejection, and pain I felt through the years. I had hoped to overcome the pesky problems that weighing me down. I wanted to forgive my father, and accept his love, but I was so disappointed.

This ordeal was a turning point in my life: something died in me that day. After I returned home, relayed my story to my mother, I fell to the floor, and in desperation I lifted my head to the Lord and cried out for help, help to ease the pain or just make it go away. I was a new convert and did not fully understand the heart of the father but, I was hopeful that some way somehow there would be change to my circumstance which would give me a new lease on life.

Although the pain of not knowing my father had a profound effect on my childhood and had somehow defined my identity, I was encouraged to mask the pain and carry on, in the hope that things would get better. I was a captive by these emotions and it would not let me go. The emotions, which followed the visit to my father's house, stirred up new emotions that I was ill-prepared to handle.

Illustration 3: Barrel and cart with rope

Chapter 3:

MY WALK WITH THE LORD

It was during one of the summer months in 1975 that a group of teenage Christians walked into my neighborhood handing out flyers and testifying about the love they found in Jesus the Christ. I had never heard such an account and piqued my interest. I had attended a Seventh-day Adventist school where the emphasis was more on the Sabbath than Jesus, I was curious to learn about a relationship with this Jesus. The teenage Christians explained to my mother that they would be at the junction in our village the upcoming Friday night to preach the gospel.

After they were through talking to Mother, I asked her if she would allow me to attend the church service. Her reply was, "As long as you complete your chores, you can go." That Friday, I took care of all my chores early enough so that I could attend the service. I was the first person at the meeting; I looked on as the crew set up their instruments and microphones in preparation to host the evening meeting. Before the meeting, the crew held hands and prayed to set the atmosphere for the evening service.

As the music began ringing through the small village, people began coming out of their houses, and very soon, the street was crowded with people from the neighborhood. The praise and worship was penetrating, but what struck me the most was a female singer whose voice was angelic. She sang a solo, "I've found the answer, and I would like to pray." My eyes were glued on her as she worshiped before the Lord. After the song, the people clapped and worshiped God along with the team of young believers. I could not help but draw close in proximity to the group of worshippers.

It was now time for the preacher to preach. He preached from John 3:16, "For God so loved the world, He gave His only begotten Son that whosoever believeth in Him shall not perish but shall have everlasting life." The preacher was dynamic and spoke the Word of God with confidence and enthusiasm that commanded the attention of the people and caused them to stay until he was through with his preaching.

At the very end of the preaching, the preacher gave an altar call. I was the first person to make it to the altar. With tears running down my cheeks, I accepted Jesus as my Lord and Savior that night. With faith in the preached Word, I felt elated and confident that something wonderful had just happened in me. I knew I was forgiven of my sins just as the preacher had said. I felt delivered from guilt and condemnation, and as though, I was given a new lease on life. I had just fallen in love with Jesus who died for me on the cross of Calvary. One of the Christian workers took my personal information at the end of the service. and I quickly made my way home. I just could not wait to share this experience with my mother and brother.

I ran through the door with a big smile on my face, and began sharing what had happened at the meeting. My mother, brother, and an extended family members listened as I explained the story. I enthusiastically shared about the singing and the preached Word. My mother's reaction was nominal, but I knew she was proud of me by the look in her eyes. She finally uttered, "I am happy for you," and hugged me. I felt so much joy!

It was difficult to fall asleep that night, it was not just because of the bed bugs, it was because of my earlier experience that evening and my new relationship with the Lord. I felt His overwhelming presence, and for the first time in my life, I knew that I was not alone; Jesus was with me and had extended to me His unconditional love.

The very next day I had an appointment with the pastor and his team. My mother allowed me to attend the meeting. While in attendance, I was given a Bible by the pastor, and he shed more light about walking with Jesus, prayer, studying the Bible, memorizing

scriptures, fasting, and baptism. The pastor insisted that he was open to questions, suggestions, and ideas during the meeting, adding that if he did not know the answer to a particular issue, he would research it and get back to me.

His openness prompted my interest as I did everyone who was present, it was obvious. At first, I was reluctant to ask questions, but I mustered up the strength and began asking questions; the pastor reciprocated with answers that made a lot of sense to me. He instructed the group to start reading the book of John in the New Testament right away, and we should not hesitate to speak to him about our concerns. The group verbalized understanding and agreed to do so.

I began reading the book of John in the car while on my way home. The experience was incredible; I could not believe the eagerness to read the Bible and what was happening within me. My mother was a staunch Catholic so what was amazing is that she had agreed for me to attend the church services. During the week, different members of the church would come to my home and take me to church, and bring back after the service. Except for a few times a week when I did not have a ride to church, I would leave my home early enough to walk to the church that was about 10 miles away from my home. Other times, I will take the area bus (my aunt would give me $2.00) if she had it. I did not want to miss a church service, it was too important to me.

I was growing in my faith and gaining an understanding of my purpose in life. The awkwardness of living in a mud house was no longer an embarrassment because I knew that God was up to something good and would turn things around. What I felt from the church members who took me back and forth to church was a deep sense of love and care. I would spend long hours reading the Scriptures and praying, I was growing stronger every day.

I would go out on Saturday mornings with the team I now was a part off to share my testimony and the Word of God with random people. I began spending less time at home and more time at the beach house which was loaned to the church. A group of believers, me included, would commit to praying and fasting on a weekly basis.

My intimacy with God catapulted as I travailed before Him, hoping to gain a better understanding of His will for my life. My mother and brother noticed the change in my life and they questioned me about it. People in the community also noticed the change and would confront my mother. Some comments were positive, others negative, but my mother and brother would always stick up for me.

There came a time when the group of six decided on a forty days prayer and fasting. Everyone in the group welcomed the idea with open arms because we read in the Word of God that Jesus fasted for forty-days and forty-nights and had triumphed over the devil. I consulted with my mother about the fast, and she supported the idea. Everyone in the group received clearance to advance.

On the fourteenth day of the fast; however, my spirit left my body. I laid there lifeless as my spirit hovered above me. I looked in at the commotion, which followed. Members of the group were crying, others praying as my lifeless body lay on the mat. They knelt and prayed with tears streaming down their faces. The registered nurse who was present instructed one of the ladies in the group to go to the kitchen and bring her a fork. The nurse took the fork and ran it up and down the soles of my feet in an effort to stimulate the nerve endings. Her best efforts were useless. A member of the group yelled, "How can we tell her mother she is dead!"

This ordeal lasted about two minutes, but it seemed like an eternity. I heard a voice saying to me, "You must return because your work is not yet done." I was reluctant to return to my body because I was in such a peaceful place. I wanted to defy the voice, but would not dare because the voice exuded such authority. Before I knew it, my spirit was back in my body. The nurse exclaimed, "I have a pulse! I have a pulse." Screams of praises to God rang through the beach house. After I pulled through, the group decided to take me home and to break the fast. I was escorted to my home by all parties present at the beach house.

The cautiously entered my home as they relayed the story, my mom shared that she felt something was wrong, she did not know the extent of it, but was making plans to get to the beach house. She was extremely happy, thanked the group, and tended to my needs. The first few sips of soup were particularly delightful. With my mother present and the care she offered I felt that I was on my way to recovery.

This situation did not deter us; we continued to do the work of the Lord. My first sermon took place in the open-air at a savannah close to the church; I was approaching eighteen years of age and had no previous experience as a preacher. My desire to have others share in the joy of salvation and be delivered from the jaws of hell was tantamount. I was not intimidated in the least. With the help of the Holy Spirit, I preached as though I was a seasoned minister of the Gospel. Many people gave their lives to Jesus that night.

I was convince that I was called to preach, so I continued preaching and teaching the gospel at every opportunity. Every Saturday morning, the group would go to the marketplace, the highways, and the byways to preach the Word and many were added to the church. We ventured to Tobago, the sister island of Trinidad, to preach the Word of God. We were not invited, so there was no one to receive us. Our going there was simply an act of faith, because we zealous for the Lord.

After exiting the boat, there was a large church in view, we walked up to the church and rang the bell. The pastor of the church opened the door and greeted us. We informed him of our mission and asked if we could spend the night at his church. Unfortunately, his response was very discouraging. He told us that faith had eyes and that we should not take chances like the ones we had taken. He strongly suggested that we return to our homes. We graciously thanked him, walked away, and continued to trust God for directions.

As we continued walking and praying, we met someone who directed us to a lady who owned houses and was also a professing believer. The lady who owned a number of houses in Tobago proposed that we stayed rent-free in one of her houses for the entire week. We were jubilant and continued to praise God. We went out every day and preach and teach the Word of God and return late in the evenings to sleep. Many souls were converted, and we encouraged them to attend Bible-believing churches where they would have the opportunity to learn and grow in their faith.

We continued in the apostles' doctrine, teaching and preaching the Word of God with much zeal. However, loneliness coupled with discouragement began setting in when most of the members of the group entering committed relationship or move outside the area to explore career opportunities; it created a sense of loneliness. I decided on getting married to escape the pain and loneliness; however, that marriage quickly ended with the death of my spouse. A couple of years had passed, and I got married to the love of my life and had two beautiful children. We moved to central Trinidad to start our new life.

> **Negative emotions started to build up in me like a stone wall. I struggled with rejection, bitterness, anger, self-hatred, loss, fear, anxiety, and rage, you name it; I experienced it. I blamed God for the heartbreak, disappointment, rejection, and pain. Although I dared not run away from Him, I slighted Him. It was no secret that I had lost my way and that the devil was quickly moving in to take advantage of my situation.**

My husband and I agreed that we should migrate to secure a better life for ourselves and daughter. I walked away from my job as a registered nurse in Trinidad, sold the furniture that we had secured for our new home, and placed my husband's brother in

the house to care for it. We packed a few suitcases and left for the United States.

While in the United States, my husband, daughter, and I encountered a different kind of hardship. People in Trinidad, like other people around the world, seek to migrate to the United States believing that America is a land flowing with milk and honey; however, to our surprise, it was quite the opposite. With little or no money in hand, menial jobs, illegal status, on-going fear of deportation, life was simply not a bed of roses.

My husband and I decided on a plan to work hard and trust God for open doors. Instead of doors being opened, it seems as though they were closing in on us. People were talking, and the devil was having a good 'ole time from our demise. However, we continue to pay the mortgage on our home in Trinidad.

In America, my family and I faithfully attended church every Sunday and would take our daughter along, but there was still so much instability in the marriage. With no stable jobs, housing issues and on-going fights, the marriage was suffering. After five years of us living in the United States, we gave birth to a son who was a welcomed addition to our family. But even during such a joyous time, I felt unloved by my husband, deep-seated loneliness, rejection and pain. Nothing seemed to be going right. My happiness seemed to be short-lived and I developed a love relationship with the thought of death which seemed overwhelmingly attractive as my faith in God dwindled.

The stories I heard over the years about my father from my mother and various relatives begin haunting me again. The thoughts never left me; they were simply dormant when I was busy with the work of the Lord. Now that I was married and had more time to sort through my thoughts, they returned with a vengeance. I can truly attest to the fact that internal and external factors can influence a person's decision making capabilities causing me to interpret things differently, words had different meaning, and everyone was a suspect.

These stories altered my emotional and functional capabilities to a great extent. I had nightmares and constant flashbacks, which resulted in anger and rage, detachment and abandonment issues, poor decision-making skills, along with feelings of low self-esteem. My past waited patiently for the opportune moment, to harass and body-hug me. I was also living a life of prayerlessness as I struggled to adjust to my marriage life. The enemy came at me with a vengeance, and eventually the marriage ended in divorce.

Chapter 4:

A SET-UP BY THE ENEMY

Demonic altars were established on both sides of my family. On my mother's side, her siblings would host an annual feast on their family grounds where they offered blood sacrifices of various animals, such as goats, sheep and chickens to different gods. They would feed the people in the community, offered prayers with loud chanting sounds, speak in strange tongues, and dance to the beat of drums into the wee hours of the morning.

My father was a notorious devil worshiper and his infamy was known throughout the community. My brother and I would listen to stories recited by our mother of him entering into his secret chamber in their home and he would not show up for hours. My mother cautiously enter the room to ask a question or express a concern, but my father would not be present.

Sometimes, she spoke of witnessing multiple snakes moving around on the bed in his secret chamber and would quickly flee the room in horror. I would listen to stories about my father vanishing from moving cars; the driver, upon realizing that he had vacated the car, would be in a quandary, sometimes fleeing their cars and running into homes for cover.

According to my mother, my father would defy the natural law of gravity by being buoyant in the air as he moved from place to place. I heard stories of him impregnating and ill-treating women while pregnant, and leaving them to raise multiple children. My mother was one of the impregnated women who were abandoned to raise her two children.

After my father's passing in 1997, I found out that I had nine siblings, beside my older brother, who shared the same father with me. My father never discussed his life, lifestyle or his multiple children with my mother, so the news of his large family took everyone by surprise. His death was very devastating to me because I never had a chance to know him. I desperately wanted to hear his side of the story. All I knew of him was what was told to me by my mother, her siblings and relatives. In the same year, I also lost my older brother (who shared the same mother and father with me) to AIDS. I felt as though my world was tragically falling apart.

The scripture in James 1:8 says that a double minded man/woman is unstable in all of his/her ways. I was that woman the bible was referencing. With the same mouth, I would bless God, curse, fuss, fight, and argue with people at the drop of a hat. James, being discerning of the double-mindedness of the people in his day, asked them a soul-searching question: "How can fresh and bitter water proceed from the same fountain," (KJV, James 3:1). This is truly a problematic question with no doubt an equally perplexing answer. I am certain that people were clandestinely posing this question, both to themselves and others, about my stance as a believer.

It was somewhere in the midst of these tumultuous situations I lost my smile. Friends and family would look at my photos and would ask, "Why are you so serious in the picture?" I would make loads of excuses, such as, "The photographer did not give me enough time to pose," or "I was not aware that the camera was on me," but deep inside, I knew the truth. I had lost the ability to smile. I would stand in front of the mirror for hours at a time and pull my cheeks from side to side in an effort to create a smile.

I would pull my checks upwards, or towards my ears but just was not able to forge a smile. I would even attempt smiling on my own, but my smile resembled that of an angry, troubled person. I forgot how to smile, and after much effort, I gave up trying.

When endorphins are produced in the brain, neuronal signals are transmitted to the facial muscles triggering a smile. However, in the orbitofrontal cortex of my brain, my sensory stimuli were repressing my ability to smile. The proof of which was seen in photos and in my interactions with others. People would ask my daughter, "Why is your mom so serious?" Even if I desperately wanted to smile, I had lost the ability to smile. I vividly recalled how I would smile so much so much as a child, and how my smile would light up a room, but it was not happening for me at this time in my life.

The hurt I carried was extremely destructive to me and others around me. It manifested itself in a number of different ways, but primarily, hurting others. There is an old adage I came to know, and I quote, "hurting people hurt people." I was reckless in my approach and had no care for the feelings of others. My words were careless and insensitive and my demeanor followed along the exact path.

My life seemed hopeless. People withdrew themselves from me when all I needed was for someone to come to my rescue, though I did not know how to ask for it. I learned a valuable lesson through this ordeal: the behaviors that some people exhibit is not always because they are immoral or evil, but more times than not, they are crying out for help. Show me a perfect man or woman who does not need help from Almighty God!

I was miserable and empty on the inside; I was crying out for help, but no one came to my rescue. When people are stand offish with others, there is one of two keys things that may be happening, they do not care, or they are too busy to care. It seemed as though everyone was engrossed in their own lives and could not take on someone else's problems. I felt as though I was quickly becoming a burden to others. Another real thought was that I had shut out a lot of people and now it was their turn to shut me out. In retrospect, I believe it was a mix of all of the above.

I began to think that I was handling the situation to the best of my ability; oddly, I was becoming callous and insensitive. The life I lived was debilitating, and grew increasingly worse over the years. As mentioned earlier, I had a sordid obsession with death. I wanted the pain to go away so I felt that death would be the

ultimate answer. I reasoned within myself that everything would come to a screeching halt if I died, and I would certainly be relieved of the pain. On several occasions, I came close to committing suicide, but for some odd reason, I just could not follow through with the plan.

In spite of the turbulence on the inside of me, I attended schools of higher education and did exceptionally well. I received honors, recognition and maintained exceptional GPA's. However, I would return to my home sad and disgusted with life. I was not able to answer this provoking question: "Who am I?" The zeal I had for the Lord when I first accepted Him as Savior had dissipated, and I was bewildered and afraid to die in that state. I did not pray, fast, or study the Word; the desire to indulge had disappeared.

I was tricked by the enemy who had a trap in place that was time-sensitive. His plan quickly came to fruition because of prayerlessness, lack of fasting and studying of God's word. I wanted the pain to go away and felt that death would be the ultimate answer.

How I was fooled by the enemy, like many believers, we are tricked into believing that God is not sovereign and does not know where we are, and what we are doing.

Hosea 4:6 says, "My people are destroyed for a lack of knowledge, because thou hast rejected knowledge, I will also reject thee, that thou shalt be no priest to me: seeing thou hast forgotten the law of thy God, I will also forget thy children." I know that the devil is shrewd and uses all forms of deception to his advantage to capture and imprison the unsuspecting. The devil's hatred towards God is robust, and since he cannot get back at Him, he is after His children. The conclusion I came to was that believers have a real adversary who is desperate to sway believers away from God. It is critical; therefore for believers to study the Word of God and hide it in their hearts so that they would not sin against Him. It is only through consistency in the Word of God that the life of God can be framed in us.

It took me a while, but once I identified the

enemy's stronghold over my life, I went to the scriptures and began studying the truth in God's word. I began studying Scriptures about God's acceptance of me and it allowed me to ambush strongholds that were sent to harass me. I untapped a scripture against every stronghold sent against me and began defeating its influence over my life. Once the devil saw that his plan was crumbling as I surrounded myself by the Word of God, submission, prayer, and fasting, his resistance began to weaken and I felt strengthen and empowerment.

Chapter 5:

DEFINING GOD

Defining God is not a simple task. People try to offer definitions, but they end up describing His attributes. Phrases such as omniscient, omnipotent, omnipresent, holy, perfect, pure, wise, to name a few, are extremely limiting when it comes to our Sovereign God. Believers are excited about sharing these attributes with others, which is plausible, but they really are not accurate descriptions of the essence of God.

This is to be expected because humans are limited by humanity and vocabulary, and really cannot embrace the magnitude of God. God is sovereign and eternal and is not limited to space or time. So, when humans attempt to describe God, they do so in ways that are familiar, but deficient in weightiness. Even attempts at describing the essence of humanity lack a clear cut definition. What ends up happening is that people continue to cite attributes. For example, to be human means to be able to think, set goals, love, hate, and interact with others in ways that are socially acceptable.

Scripture gives believers a biblical framework about what God is like and how we can know him. Exploring this framework empowers believers to better understand who He is. God is not a man, but a Spirit. Man is a created being and although he has unique attributes, God has attributes that man does not possess. It is also a fact that man was made in God's image (Genesis 1: 26-28) and shares attributes with God; man is finite, God is infinite.

As picturesque as the descriptions of God seem to be to humans, they are simply attributes and do not speak to the essence of God. Although, the inability to describe the essence of God is usually

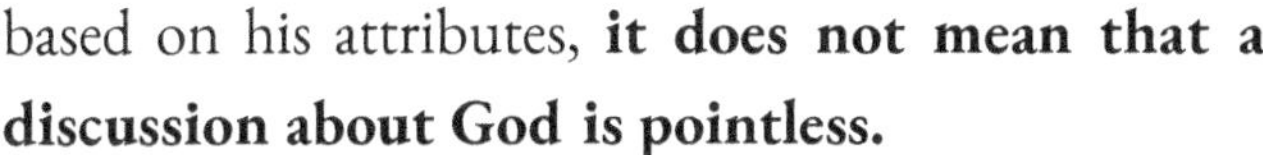

based on his attributes, **it does not mean that a discussion about God is pointless.**

Becoming a Christian does not mean following a set of rules or adopting a feel-good philosophy that tags an unrealistic view of one's self. Christianity is all about having a relationship with God. John 3:16 says, "For God so loved the world that He gave His only begotten Son that whosoever believes in Him shall not perish but have everlasting life."

John 1:12 KJV says, "But as many as received Him, to them he gave power to become the sons of God, even to them that believe in His name," which means we must believe that Jesus Christ died on the cross for the forgiveness of our sins.

Atheists often ask Christians to define God not by attributes, but His essence; believers fail because of the limitation of the human mind. When Christians fail in their attempts to define the essence of God, atheists find an occasion to insult our faith. In reality, atheists are faced with the same dilemma when asked to define humanity; they quickly ignore or change the topic. The bottom line is that they are subtly attempting to deny God and His existence.

I endorse, if it is permissible for atheists to ask Christians to define God without the use of attributes, then it should be equally acceptable to ask an atheist to define his humanity. Not being able to describe the essence of God without citing his attributes does not mean that a discussion about God is pointless.

The "Essence of God" is a theological term that is used to refer to God's personal characteristics, or to the facets of His personality. Sometimes the term "Attributes of God" is interchangeably used to refer to God's essence. The essence of God is primary characteristics that cannot be completely communicated by man. His characteristics can be described to a degree, but they cannot be fully defined because finite man cannot define the infinite.

God approaches every issue regarding human beings out of His love for us and utilizes all of His attributes into consideration of us. His overarching

feature is love, He is always gracious, and always thinks from a standpoint of grace.

Can Believers Experience God?

This is a difficult question because the answer can be rather subjective. The generalized view of love is elation, euphoria, and joy. According to the Bible, love is not so much of a feeling but a commitment. 2 Corinthians 13 says, "Love is kind; it is not easily provoked and is not selfish." Simply put, love is more about giving than receiving.

Experiencing God has little to do with feelings, but everything to do with servant hood. The greatest example of selflessness is seen in the person of Jesus Christ. He loved the world, so instead of allowing humanity to face judgment for their sin, Jesus paid the ultimate sacrifice on the cross for us. John 15:13 stresses, the greatest act of love was when He laid down His life for His friends. To experience God's love is to accept His Son through faith, continue in His word, and live according to His commands. It also means spending time knowing and appreciating His presence. Only then, will a person experience God's love and protection over their lives.

Walking with God is humbling because it totally changes a person. When a believer learns what it means to enter into God's presence, change takes place from the inside out. It causes a person to see themselves as they really are. Because God is love, He embraces us, and He teaches us how to embrace Him. Basking in God's presence is a profound experience. There is nothing like it. It is a humbling experience and is extremely overwhelming. Christians everywhere ought to appreciate God's presence; His presence is awesome!

More believers need to come into God's presence. He has given us an open invitation. Hebrew 4:16 says, "Let us therefore come boldly unto the throne of grace, that we may obtain mercy, and find grace to help in time of need." Believers must get acquainted to God's awe, wonder, and the irresistible greatness of His presence. It is dangerous to worship Him from

afar. God has made an investment in His people and He is looking for a return on His investment. Give Him praise and glory!

Chapter 6:

DEMONS AND THEIR ABILITIES

Demons are evil spirits that are opposed to God and His people. The primary references in the New Testament are found in 2 Pet. 2:4 and in the book of Jude 6. Included below are references in the New Testament about demonic oppressions:

- Matt. 4:24, "And the news about Him went out into all Syria; and they brought to Him all who were ill, taken with various diseases and pains, demoniacs, epileptics, paralytics; and He healed them."

- Matt. 8:28, "And when He had come to the other side into the country of the Gadarenes, two men who were demon-possessed met Him as they were coming out of the tombs; they were so exceedingly violent that no one could pass by that road."

- Mark 3:22, "And the scribes who came down from Jerusalem were saying, 'He is possessed by Beelzebul,' and "He casts out the demons by the ruler of the demons."

- Luke 4:35, "And Jesus rebuked him, saying, "Be quiet and come out of him! "And when the demon had thrown him down in their midst, he came out of him without doing him any harm."

- John 8:48-49, "The Jews answered and said to Him, "Do we not say rightly that you are a Samaritan and have a demon?" Jesus answered, "I do not have a demon; but I honor My Father, and you dishonor me."

Demons are spiritual beings without physical form. They were probably created before the world was and like Satan, fell away from God. Revelations 12:4 is a reference to a third of the angels falling who are referred to as demons.

The term "demon" comes from the Greek "daimon" Demons are found in the New Testament as having the ability to possess humans (Matt. 8:28-34; Mark 5:1-4) and animals (Matt. 8:32). Demons are also strong (Mark 5:4). They are called unclean spirits (Luke 8:29), have a chain of command in their demonic realm (Matt. 12:24-27), and can have sacrifices offered to them (1 Cor. 10:20).

Ultimately, demons will be judged in the future (Matt. 8:29) and most importantly, they cannot be redeemed. The apostle Paul was sensitive to demonic forces and their underpinnings and referred to them as principalities (Rom. 8:38). He pointed out that believers are in a struggle against them in Ephesians 6:11-12 and that they operate in heavenly places. However, as children of God, we must always remember that we are seated in Heavenly places above principalities and powers, which gives us the advantage.

There is a debate among Christians as to exactly what demons are. Some say that they are fallen angels that were originally created by God but who rebelled against Him and followed Lucifer (Satan). Others say that they could be the released spirits of the Nephilim; that they were the offspring of the "sons of God" and the "daughters of men."

Genesis 6:1-2 says, "Now it came about, when men began to multiply on the face of the land, and daughters were born to them, that the sons of God saw that the daughters of men were beautiful; and they took wives for themselves, whomever they chose."

One possibility is that the "sons of God" are the fallen angels who took human form and had relations with women, and their offspring were called the Nephilim. The idea behind this theory is that since the Messiah was to be born by a virgin, Lucifer sought to undermine his birth by corrupting the human line with fallen angels becoming intimate with women. But, here is my argument--Noah's generation was purged after the flood which means that this theory has some serious flaws.

Following this theory was that of Sethite, where both Christians and Jews believed that the "sons of God" were the offspring of Seth. Whether or not demons are the result of interbreeding between angels and women or they are simply fallen angels, demonic forces are powerful and very capable. Following is a list of their demonic activities:

1. They can possess people (Matt. 8:16- 28, 15:22, Mark 1:32, Mark 7:26).
2. Multiple demons can live in a person at a time (Mark 5:9-12, Mark 16:9, Luke 8:2, Luke 8:27 and 30).
3. The devil wants God's people to offer sacrifices to himself (Lev. 17:7; Deut. 32:17; Psalm 106:37; 1 Cor. 10:20).
4. Demons can speak (Matt. 8:31; Mark 5:12; Luke 4:33-34, 41).
5. Demons can cause muteness (Matt. 9:32-33; Luke 11:14).
6. Demons can cause blindness (Matt. 12:22).
7. Demons can cause lunacy (Matt. 17:15-18; Luke 4:35).

8. Demons can cause self-harm (Matt. 17:15-18; Luke 4:35).

9. Demons can dwell in animals (Mark 5:12-13; Luke 8:32-33).

10. Demons can move people to be naked (Luke 8:27).

11. Demons can move people to dwell in tombs (Luke 8:27).

12. Demons can move people to dwell in the desert (Luke 8:30).

13. Demons can induce seizures (Luke 9:42).

14. Demons can spread their doctrines or beliefs (1 Tim. 4:1).

15. Demons are knowledgeable of God (James 2:19).

16. Demons love promoting their wisdom (James 3:15).

17. Demons love to receive worship (Rev. 9:20).

18. Demons occupy geographical regions (Rev. 18:2).

Based on the Scriptures, demonic forces have a wide array of capabilities. Of course, their ultimate goal is to deceive and separate human-kind from God.

As Christians; however, we do not have to fear the demonic realm because greater is He that is in each and every one of us than he that is in the world (1 John 4:4). Remember, in the Gadarene, Jesus cast out the devil and the man was able to fulfill his calling. The Bible says that God has given believers power to tread upon serpents and scorpions and over all the wiles of the enemy.

What Opens Up Believers to Demonic Oppression?

In Ephesians 6:12, believers come into an understanding of the war with demons and how they are organized to bring defeat to God's people. The fact of the matter is that a Christian cannot be demon-possessed, but one can be oppressed. Believers, without realizing it, often open themselves to demonic oppression. Demonic oppression is the attack by demonic forces that often results in illness, depression, financial difficulty, and abnormal fear, to name a few. It is a good idea to be mindful of things that can give access to spiritual oppression:

- Past involvement in occult activity- occult activity includes Ouija boards, tarot cards, astrology, séances, necromancy (contacting the dead), and divination.

- Past involvement in false religion- doctrines of demons (1 Tim. 4:1; Matt. 24:24). To dabble in them is to directly dabble in demonic activity. Such false religions would be Mormonism, Jehovah's Witness, Islam, Roman Catholicism, etc.

- Drug use- usage alters the state of the mind and can invite demonic activity since it promotes the loss of control of the mind as well as denying God's intention for us to be sober-minded. The Greek word for sorcery is *pharmakeia*, from which the word pharmacy is derived (Galatians 5:20; Revelation 9:21; 18:23).

- Pornography- a sin of lust that can easily open a person up to having demonic influences and control.

- Occult meditation techniques- emptying the mind, centering prayer, and repetition.

Chapter 7:

WISDOM IS PRINCIPAL IN THE WAR AGAINST THE DEVIL

You may ask the question, "What is wisdom?" The Bible's definition of wisdom is the fear of the Lord. When a person fears God, in return he or she receives guidance and direction for his life and family. In 1 Corinthians 3:19, the Bible labels the wisdom of this world as foolishness. Real wisdom is found in obedience and reverence to God and His Word. The Bible also says that if any man lacks wisdom, he should ask God who will freely give it.

The Beginning and End of Wisdom

Wisdom begins with reverence toward God. It is a deep, abiding respect for the Lord and His Word. If you have never spent time in the book of Proverbs, my advice is that you should. This book gives believers an insight into the life of Solomon, who, before Jesus, was the wisest man on Earth. Proverbs 9:10 says, "The fear of the Lord is the beginning of wisdom, and the knowledge of the Holy One is insight." Respect breeds obedience, and obedience pleases God. God said it Himself in Hosea 6:6 that He prefers obedience rather than sacrifice.

Obedience follows understanding, which is preceded by wisdom. When a believer obeys what they know to be true, it pleases God, and their vocation becomes easy. Where there is no fear of God, there is limits to His wisdom. James 1:5-6 says, "If any of you lack wisdom, ask God who gives generously to all without finding fault, and it shall be given to him. But when you ask, you must believe and not doubt, because the one who doubts is like a wave of the sea, blown and tossed by the wind."

The follow-up question is, "Why do believers need wisdom?" 1 Peter 5:8 warns believers that the devil walks around seeking all those whom he may devour. Now, listen to a father's instructions to his son in the book of Proverbs: "Do not forsake wisdom, she will preserve you; love her and she will guard you. Wisdom is supreme; therefore acquire wisdom. And whatever else you obtain, gain understanding. Prize her, and she will exalt you; if you embrace her, she will honor you."

This father is instructing his son in the ways of wisdom possibly because of his own experience with the Lord. We see here that wisdom is not intelligence or knowledge; it is the ability to come into a full understanding of acquired information. I refer to this type of wisdom as divine intelligence. It is significant for believers to ask God for wisdom, but they should also gain understanding to implement it. The Bible encourages believers to gain understanding above all else.

I must stress that wisdom cannot be gleaned from a book because books only provide us with knowledge. Knowledge also does not have the ability to make a person wise. What people need is the spiritual insight to think and act in ways that are profitable, stimulate good judgment, and productivity.

When Solomon became king, he asked God for wisdom instead of material things. God not only granted the desire of his heart, but He also replied, "Since you have asked for this and not for long life or wealth for yourself, nor have asked for the death of your enemies, but for discernment in administering justice, I will do what you have asked. I will give you a wise and discerning heart, so that there will never have been anyone like you, nor will there ever be" (1 Kings 3:11). Solomon's wisdom grew so great that his fame spread abroad and the Queen of Sheba paid him a visit to witness his wisdom.

The Apostle James asked a rhetorical question: "Who is wise and understanding among you?" The answer he gave was equally pompous. He said, "By his good conduct let him show his works in the meekness of wisdom" (James 3:13). James also revealed the difference between earthly wisdom and godly wisdom by saying, "The wisdom from above is first pure, then peaceable, gentle, open to reason, full of mercy and good fruit, impartial and sincere," (James 3:17). However, the wisdom of the world is folly with God (1 Corinthians 3:19).

Jesus told his disciples in Luke 21:25, "I will give you a mouth and wisdom which none of your adversaries will be able to withstand or contradict." This is a powerful statement because what Jesus was certainly alluding to was He is the source of wisdom. The Bible says in Proverbs 29:3, "He who loves wisdom makes his father glad."

In the warfare against the devil, wisdom is the key. Wisdom embodies strategy. Proverbs 28:6

instructs the believer, "Whosoever trusts in his own strength is a fool, but he who walks in wisdom will be delivered for it is by wisdom a house is built and by wisdom it is established." The weight of wisdom is seen again in Solomon's statement in Proverbs 23:23, "Buy the truth, and sell it not: also wisdom, and instruction, and understanding." Saints, every other truth except the wisdom of God is destined to fail.

Chapter 8:

HOW I REGAINED MY SMILE

I was lying on my bed one day, physically, emotionally, and spiritually drained by the overwhelming oppression of demonic influences. I began a conversation with the Lord asking for His forgiveness, strength, and wisdom to live for Him. I was wounded and practically left for dead, and the devil, my nemesis, was totally amused by my demise. After the prayer, I felt an immediate sense of relief and strength. It was at that moment that I decided to surrender to the Lord completely and submit to His authority. Like the prodigal son, the Father took me in, put a ring on my finger, and clothed me with His love and compassion.

As I mentioned earlier, I was known as the child who always wore a big smile that filled up a room. Smiling came naturally to me, it was my trademark. As a child, life was free from care, and worry; not that there weren't problems but because the problems did not matter to me. My mother and brother handled it. As a result, I was a spontaneous and happy-go-lucky child and wanted everyone around me to know about it. What I did not realize was that the devil, the adversary, was sizing me up and would use past circumstances to oppress and detour me.

I never fully realized the extent of my hardship as a child and the impact it would have on my life. I would be embarrassed when my friends spoke about their dads or discussed a TV show, but by and large, I was a happy and content child. As mentioned before, I cannot remember the particular moment in time when the actual change took place in my ability to smile, but it happened and it left me with a flat affect that was quite a contrast.

As I continued down the path of prayerlessness, and refusal to study the Word of God, I longed to regroup, but I could not find my way. I felt as if someone or something had pushed me so far away from his presence. The force was evil, willful, and measured, even time-sensitive in nature.

When the devil finds a Christian who is not at his or her post or is just simply playing church, he seizes that opportunity and moves in to oppress, harass, and depress that individual in the most violent way to keep them away from their purpose. It is no secret that the devil hates God, but because God is untouchable, His children who are not fully committed or consistent to the Lord are at his advantage.

Prior to me crying out to the Lord, I would envision destruction, hopelessness, emotional harassment, and fear. I wanted the Lord to help me recover from the satanic strongholds I was experiencing but was too ashamed and afraid to reach out for help. Oftentimes, I would feel as if someone or something was physically bruising and crushing me, condemning me, and applying extreme pain and pressure to my person. The pain was intractable and I wanted it off me.

I would remember how I used to pray and fast and spend long hours in worship, but I felt that God had forgotten and forsaken me. Because I felt defeated, I refrained from talking to Him. I was physically, emotionally, and spiritually stagnated.

Although I missed the presence of God and I knew that He had missed fellowshipping with me, the numbness and pain that I felt over the years had far-reaching effects on me and created a whirlwind of problems that I did not anticipate. It not only affected me but the lives of others around me.

I longed for the richness, beauty, and presence of the Lord, but I ignored and disregarded His loving embrace. I wanted the life God had for me, but pride kept me from realizing it. For some odd reason, I was ready to exchange my pain for His peace. Staying in that isolated position was no longer my ambition or a choice.

As I lay on my bed in humility and brokenness contemplating the decision I made, I felt the overwhelming presence of God, not physically, but within my heart. His presence did not bear judgment; neither was it punitive. It was warm, immensely loving, and kind. His presence filled the space, and with no words uttered, I knew I was in the presence of a big God who loved me so.

It was a *kairos* moment, which is a precise and delicate moment in time that offers a unique opportunity. God the Father had caught up with me. I did not have the strength nor the wherewithal to run anymore; mercy and grace had engulfed me, and I surrendered to its Lordship. I responded by seizing the moment which was transformational in nature.

Based on the many testimonials I have heard over the years, although there are some similarities with visitations from God, it is safe to say that He manifests differently to His children based on our needs. God's presence is as unique as it is individualized. His love goes beyond mere feelings. The best way I can describe His presence is that it was a knowing deep within the recesses of my heart that someone greater than me was in the room. His presence was accompanied by lightness, peace, joy, and transference of strength and confidence. As you may imagine, this encounter is difficult to describe because of the limitations of the English language.

The reason why believers do not experience God on a day-to-day basis is that they fail to tune in to His frequency. To get God's opinion about the simple realities around them, believers need to be in-sync with the Holy Spirit. The Bible says that His sheep know His voice, and the voice of a stranger they will not follow. In contrast, a carnal man is not in tune with God and is neither hot nor cold.

Oftentimes, we hear Christians testify about being in God's presence. As we are well aware through the teaching of the Scriptures, God's presence is everywhere. The Bible references God's presence in Heaven, at particular locations, such as Jerusalem, and in the lives of those who make Jesus Christ the Lord of their lives. Believers often testify that His presence was at a church service on a Sunday morning or at Bible study. God is omnipresent, He can be everywhere at every time because He is God. So what does it really mean when we say, "I was in God's presence?"

Let us explore the scriptures, John 14:26 states that true worship is possible because the Holy Spirit lives within the heart of every believer and therefore, believers can be in constant communion with God; it does not have to wait for a convenient time or place. It is no longer necessary for believers to travel to sacred places in search of His presence. God's presence is resident with us.

Although the internal change happened immediately, the outward change was gradual and went unnoticed for quite a while. But with the help of the Holy Spirit, who made the shift people began to notice, and made positive comments. I was regaining my confidence and embracing my future with the help of the Holy Spirit. God's love was overwhelmingly mind-boggling and metamorphic. Submission to God was a welcomed and liberating change; my past no longer had a hold on me. I was being made free.

Spending time in God's presence was as beautiful as it was enriching. I could not get enough of His presence. I would steal away during the day while at work to hurry past everyone to the bathroom to tell Him how much I loved Him. The psalmist David's description of the Word is so fitting. He said, "It is sweeter than honey and the honeycomb" (Psalm 19: 10).

I continued to dwell in the presence of God, my praise, worship, and prayers were genuine. I was redeveloping a relationship with the Lord, and I loved it. I desired to know Him in his fullness and be transformed into His image. I believed with all my whole heart when a man or woman prays, God is attentive to answer their prayer. I pressed on as I encouraged myself with the words from our Brother Paul: "I press toward the mark for the prize of the high calling of God in Christ Jesus" (Phil. 3:14), "looking unto Jesus the author and finisher of (my) faith" (Heb. 12:2).

I cannot recall the reason for an outburst of joy and happiness, but I found myself singing, praising, and dancing in my bathroom. It was an overflow of peace and contentment, and it felt good. I looked into the mirror and began smiling at my childish self as I pranced around the bathroom floor.

As I peered in the mirror, I realized I had been smiling, and my smile was from ear to ear. I could not believe what I was seeing. I began smiling all the more, and with tears running down my cheek, I worshiped the Lord. I exclaimed as loudly as I could, "My smile is back; it is finally back!" For the next hour, I refused to stop myself from smiling back and forth in the mirror. The Lord had surely turned my frown into a smile.

I want to propose to my readers that failure is not a death sentence; you are just one opinion shy of your divine destiny. God will restore whatever the devil stole from you as you continue to walk before Him in uprightness. He is truly a restorer of the breach and deserves true worship.

I am assuming that you may have been tempted several times while reading this book to measure your life with mine, but your measurement should not bear weight. God is the one who balances the scale and gives the desired outcome. It is important to note that God has the final word in every situation. It is inherent in human nature to judge one another, but Matthew 7:1 encourages us not to judge lest we be judged.

Sin must be dealt with by leaders in the local church and should never be swept underneath a rug; however, this Scripture is often misinterpreted. It has been marshaled to defend oneself against wrong-doing. This is not the intention here. I had sinned; I did wrong both to man and to the Lord. The devil had gotten permission from God to afflict me, but like the Gadarene demoniac in the Bible, the Lord had a set time for my deliverance.

I am reminded of the Scripture in Psalm 30:5, "For His anger is but for a moment, His favor is for life, weeping may endure for a night, but joy comes in the morning." The Father had never left me. I listened to my emotions and pain rather than trusting Him. I was the one who walked away, thinking that I would be better off on my own.

The devil lied to me, and I believed him, only to realize, just as the Bible says, that the devil is the father of lies. I am so grateful for God's unchanging love towards His children. Psalm 34:18 has been my stay, "The Lord is close to the brokenhearted and saves those who are crushed in spirit."

As you read this book, my guess is that you may be experiencing different emotions and have lots of questions. You may have been moved to tears, laid the book down, picked it up again, or even whispered a prayer. Some may have detached themselves from my story since there was no semblance to their own; others simply cannot relate. I understand. God, the Father, has made us different, and our vocation is as individual as it is God- ordained.

It is my guess that you have been through trials or periods of discouragement in your life, here is my advice: do not give up. For those who have never experienced any trouble or trial, do not boast or get careless in your walk with God. Build yourself in the Word, pray and fast because trials will come. They will come to make you strong.

The Lord has reassured us that if we are not tempted, we are none of His. I am confident that I am not the only believer who has experienced or will experience disillusionment. I felt that my story is compelling enough to write this book so that when you come under attack by the devil, you will be reminded of the love of God and embrace the courage needed to withstand every temptation. I encourage you to rest in the unlimited love of your Father and smile.

Chapter 9:

TRUE WORSHIP

Worship is not singing slow songs, singing aloud, praise dancing, lifting hands, or even kneeling. Also, it is not the amount of money a believer places in the offering basket or his or her participation at the church. These undertakings are expressions of worship but do not define true worship. As I studied the meaning of worship, I came across several definitions. Webster's Dictionary defines worship as "Honor with extravagant love and extreme submission." This definition is very appealing to me because it summarizes the priority that must be placed on worship.

True worship addresses the priority a believer places on who God is in their lives. We all have a list of priorities, some on paper, and others in our minds, but if God is not first on our list of priorities, we have failed miserably and cannot consider ourselves true worshippers. True worship is a heart condition that expresses itself through a lifestyle of obedience to God.

A lifestyle of obedience releases an extravagant love for God. It will cause you to get up early and lie down late. People will jeer at you and call you names like fanatic or "holy roller," to name a few, but it will not matter to you. You will be misunderstood and rejected and may even find yourself in isolation or without friends, but it would not deter you. True worship stems from a selfless desire to please God, not only in word but in deeds, and should be a non-negotiable priority in our lives.

Many people, believers included are worshiping an unknown God. You may question this statement, but unless the Lord is seated on the throne of our hearts, unless He is first, unless there is a constant communion with Him, He is unknown to us. Do you remember when you first met that special someone in your life? Every waking moment was spent thinking of him or her, talking to them, or just desiring to be in their presence. The same is true with God; you must desire Him.

Children of God, I admonish you to worship God, He is Lord and Savior. He purchased us with His blood, rescuing us from the penalty of sin. His sacrifice was extreme, and as if that was not enough, He declared us righteous and asked the question, "Who can lay a charge to my elect?" In a modern sense, Jesus' death was a form of bartering or exchange; the big difference of this exchange was disproportionate in that Jesus gave his righteousness for our sins. The Bible says, for God so loved the world, that He gave his only begotten Son to die in our place so that we may have eternal life (John 3:16).

Our extravagant love for God should flow from the fact that He loved us first and gave Himself for us. It is appropriate to thank God for the things He has done for us, but true worship is not based on things but on the person of Jesus Christ. Things are by-products of His grace. Often, Christian leaders and members alike are tempted to equate cars, houses, husbands, wives, and children with God's approval in their lives when what God desires from us is true worship from the heart. We cannot continue to *put the cart before the horse*. Worship will open the door for the things you desire, but true worship of God must be our priority.

Psalm 96:5-6 declares, "For all the gods of the nations are idols: but the Lord made the heavens. Honor and majesty are before him: strength and beauty are in his sanctuary." True worship must be ascribed to Him, who is worthy. None can be compared to Him; He is the uncreated Creator, King of kings, and Lord of Lords. He is not our neighborhood ATM situated for our convenience; He is omnipotent, omnipresent, and omniscient. *I feel a praise right here!*

One writer says, "We must focus our practice of worship on the worthiness of God and not his wealthiness." The Bible says that the cattle on a thousand hills belong to God, and that the streets of Heaven are paved with gold. Our Heavenly Father has unusual riches, but for His people to parallel His riches with His sovereignty is totally disrespectful and must be prioritized.

If God refuses to bless you, shower you with gifts and meet all your wants and needs, would you still worship Him? What is your motive for worship? Am I making myself clear when I said that true worship does not have any strings attached to it? True worship does not need a cheerleader, orchestra, piano, guitar, or drums; it is a spontaneous and voluntary offering to God. It is pure and genuine because of a deep-seated understanding of who He is. The conclusion of the matter is that those who know Him will worship Him.

Because God responds to us through worship, worship has been misunderstood because we equate worship with receiving. Instead, worship is all about giving, giving of our presence, heart, and time to God.

We expect God to be at our disposal and when He does not respond accordingly, we are impatient, anxious, and discouraged. It is no fault of God's; it is our own. God cannot be coerced because He is God. He answers in His own time and volition. Stop looking for a pie in the sky or manna on your lawn. Work out your salvation with fear and trembling. God will come in His own time as we remain faithful.

Believers must habitually practice living from the inside out. In Romans 12:1, Paul refers to this type of worship as "spiritual worship." Psalm 96 declares, "Let all creation rejoice before the Lord, for He comes, He comes to judge the Earth. He will judge the world in righteousness and the peoples in His faithfulness." God is coming back for a church without spot or wrinkle, those who have made a commitment to value and treasure Him above all else in true worship.

Jesus said in Matthew 15:8-9, "These people honor me with their lips, but their heart is far from me: in vain do they worship." He was making an analogy, as subtle as it is, but profound in nature. There is a kind of worship that pleases God, and then there is another type of worship that does not please Him. What we find in our churches is that people are offering lip service without heart or commitment. God is appalled by it and does not consider it. He has an all-or-nothing principle when it comes to worship.

I would like to go a bit deeper to help my readers come to a better understanding of the meaning of true worship. Jesus gave the perfect example when He said in John 4:23-24, "The hour is coming, and now is when the true worshiper will worship me in Spirit and in truth. For the Father is seeking such people to worship Him." God is a Spirit, and spirit worship reverberates with His Spirit. Worship must be authentic and pure. Flesh and soul worship are an abomination to the Lord. A spiritual connection must be made where our human spirits connect with the Spirit of God as we stand in awe of Him.

Our worship must be driven by the truth of who He is. If a believer has never come into the revelation of who God is, he or she cannot consider themselves a true worshipper. True worship comes with an understanding of the truth of God. The essence of true worship is the response of the heart to the value of His infinite worth and beauty. Worship was designed to put God's supreme worth on display.

The summary of true worship is found in the book of Hebrews 13:15-16. It says, "Through Him then, let us continually offer up the sacrifice of praise to God, that is, the fruit of lips that acknowledge His name. Do not neglect to do good and to share what you have, for such sacrifices are pleasing to God." We see that God clearly pointed out acts of worship in this Scripture: first, the fruits of our lips that acknowledge His name and our diligence in doing good and sharing what we have with others.

Romans 12:1 says, "I appeal to you, therefore, by the mercies of God, present your bodies as a living sacrifice, holy and acceptable, which is your reasonable service." Everything that we do in this body is accounted for. When we love one another, we are displaying the worth of God in our lives, and He is pleased with our contributions as worshippers.

The essence of worship is getting to know God and responding to Him from our hearts by valuing Him. Valuing God is to respect, esteem, and treasure Him and be pleased with Him above every earthly possession. The Bible says that there remains a rest for the people of God, the rest from knowing He is our God. He will not leave us nor forsake us. It is acquiring and maintaining satisfaction in God's abiding presence and sovereignty.

My experience has humbled me and has caused me to see the Lord as Ruler and Master over my life. It was good for me that I was afflicted because it has worked in me a life of gratitude and contentment. I am no longer just a girl with a smile but a woman with a heart and tenacity to do the will of God. The devil is forbidden to touch my body in any way, form, or fashion. He is forbidden to touch my smile or my happiness. My smile is permanent and will continue to shine forth as I touch hurting people around the world.

I renounce every demonic assignment and altars that have been set up by my forefathers for the boosting and elevation of evil agendas. I abort and destroy lines of communication with my name, family, and children's names on them. All the underpinnings of demonic activities are brought to a sudden halt as I return them to their sender in the mighty name of Jesus the Christ. I command all time-sensitive demonic plots and schemes to be capsized by the power that works in me. Amen and praises to my God!

A PRAYER OF SALVATION

If you would like to become a true worshiper, then you must first admit that you are in need of a Savior.

Read the following Scriptures aloud:

- Romans 3:10-12- "There is no one righteous, not even one; there is no one who understands; there is no one who seeks God. All have turned away; they have together become worthless; there is no one who does good not even one."

Put your trust in God, for He is your only hope:

- John 3:16- "For God so loved the world that He gave His only begotten son that whosoever believes in Him shall not perish, but have everlasting life."

- John 1:2- "To all who will receive Him, to them He will give power to become the sons of God."

Now confess Jesus as you Lord:

Dear Jesus,

I recognize that I am a sinner in need of a Savior, according to Romans 3:10-12. You saw my needs, and you came down from Heaven, put on flesh, and died in my place. I receive you as my Lord and Savior. Wash me in your precious blood, cleanse me from my sin and give me the power, according to John 1:12, to become your son (or daughter) in the mighty name of Jesus Christ. Amen.

PRAYER OF RECOMMITMENT AND SURRENDER

Dear God,

I confess that I have strayed from my first love, which is you, Jesus. I want to recommit my life to you. Please help me to become the person you created me to be. I want to always live a life that is pleasing to you. I want to be a witness to others and to share with them your saving grace and power. Forgive me for taking control of my life. I want you to be the Lord of my life.

Renew my passion for walking closely with you. You know all my desires and plans. Help me to fulfill your unique call and purpose in my life. Renew my heart, restore the joy of my salvation, and grant me a willing spirit to sustain my walk with you. Lord, thank you for the hope I have in you. Use my life to bring glory, honor, and praise to your name. Thank You, Lord Jesus, for hearing and answering my prayer.

Amen and Praise the Lord!

www.ingramcontent.com/pod-product-compliance
Lightning Source LLC
Chambersburg PA
CBHW052105150726
48002CB00006B/2233